Seasons and Musings

RACHAEL ROXANNE VAUGHN

Copyright © 2022 by Rachael Roxanne Vaughn

All rights reserved.

No portion of this book may be reproduced in any form without written permission from the publisher or author, except as permitted by U.S. copyright law.

This book is dedicated to:

My children, Sabrina and Isadore, who inspire me and save me every day. This book is only possible because they have kept me firmly planted on this earth. I hope this book inspires them to chase their dreams!

My sis, who first taught me unconditional love when she came into my world and whose face I saw in my darkest hour, which gave me the strength to fight for another day.

My mom who instilled a love of reading and writing in me by reading to me every night when I was little. She is my rock and my best friend and gives so much of herself to help me.

Joseph Gordon-Levitt, who created a site called HitRecord with his brother, that helped me to re-capture my passions and dreams that were once stolen from me. Because of him, I found my voice again and expanded my creative horizons. This was a life-affirming and life-changing place for me, so I thank him with the depths of my soul.

Twenty One Pilots, whose music gave me life and joy and enabled me to see that life was worth fighting for, that I was worth fighting for.

Brandi Carlile, whose music kept me sane and safe through very dark times.

Elizabeth Gilbert, whom I adore and who taught me through her writing to live "creatively beyond fear."

Christine Pacheco, my therapist, who saved my life through her kindness, love, care, and belief in me.

I would like to thank:

Esther Leon, my soul sister and one of my oldest friends, for inspiring such beautiful art for my book cover and for her enduring love and friendship! May all our dreams come true!

Victoria and T Savo for not only lending their incredible talents to help me self-publish but also for encouraging me to trust myself and my abilities.

The people, artists, movies, music, and magic of life that has inspired me, made me laugh, made me cry, and made me grateful to be alive!

Contents

WINTER 1

1. Depression 2
2. A Tear's Journey 4
3. Rêver 6
4. Something More 8
5. Surrender 11
6. Fade 13
7. Escape 15
8. It's Relative 17

9. Trapped	19
10. Tired	21
11. Enough	22
12. Glass Box	24
13. Closure	25
14. Yummy	27
15. Words Unsaid	29
SPRING	33
16. Love Is	34
17. You	36
18. Immemorial	38
19. Disappearing Act	41
20. Compassion	43
21. You and I	46
22. Daughter	48
23. New	49

24. Eternal	51
25. Beautiful	53
SUMMER	55
26. Summer	56
27. Cloud 19	57
28. The Orb	58
29. What is This?	60
30. Here	62
31. Learn	64
32. Acceptance	66
33. Existence	68
34. Inner Child	69
35. Home	71
FALL	73
36. Only Now	74
37. That Life	76

38.	In The Box	78
39.	Whispers	80
40.	A Moment of Truth	82
41.	Wishing	84
42.	I Forgot	85
43.	Birthday	87
44.	Who, Me?	89
45.	Waiting	91
46.	Perseverance	93
47.	Interruption	95
48.	Cherish	97
49.	Paper Fragments	99
50.	Becoming You	101

WINTER

1

Depression

Ugh
This weight
This suffocation
This humidity
Now a web
Engulfs
I push here
I pull there
Nothing and
Everything

All at once
It's tremendous
Impulses
Intrusion
Introspection
Too much
Always
Too much
These feelings
Please leave

2
A Tear's Journey

Another tear is born
Child of pain and love
Wrought from hidden depths
For what does it mourn?
Traveling the fractured path alone
Down, down, always down
Knowing there shall be no solace
In memories it scorns to own
For here an old friend is no more
Alive, yet dead as he was

Now a haunting nightmare
Unable to love as he swore
Did you not show me good?
I adored you, I loved you
But now who were you?
This ghost I do not know as I should
Companions now join the sojourner
A flood of rage, another of sorrow
The best friends of heartbreak
To this, the tear is no foreigner

3

Rêver

Is that you I see?
Is that your voice?
I search for you in my dreams
Are you looking for me?
I do not have a choice
Yes, a figure in the gray
Why did you go? It cries
The words echo as I drift off
How could I even stay?
There was no time for goodbyes

Nameless and faceless you are
Shadows of those I knew
Just the past haunting the night
To stay was worse by far
Peace to be had only if I flew
But it was a false hope
I loved you as you were
To these wanderings there'll be no end
With this pain I cannot cope
Only of that, am I sure

4

Something More

It is not for me
This life
With all its trimmings
How to make them see?
Never satisfied
On to the next best thing
Seeking happiness in all that is material
For something more, have they never tried?
Attention grabbed, attention lost

Who's in the spotlight now?

They want more, more, more

But do they ever count the cost?

Truth? It does not exist

Integrity? You must be joking!

Innocence? Who wants that?

Another meaningless fling? Can't resist

How does one play this game?

Where true love has no place

In which hearts have no value

And each new one is just another name

Have fun, it is the only way

Do not care, for they don't

Oh silly naive one

All you need is another lay

Do you not want pleasure?

Here, it is all yours

Now, in this moment

Come, it is your time of leisure
It is powerful indeed
This longing, this needing
At times, all-consuming
When shall I be freed?
Emptiness in all I see
Vain to the last drop
Where is the love I seek?
Yes this life is not for me

5

Surrender

I am suffocating, unable to draw breath

The walls are closing in

I am drowning beneath an ocean of lies, betrayal, and pain

I am falling with no landing in sight

I am tired, so tired, of striving for nothing, waiting

I have lost the will to fight

I will walk the lonely road to the end and let no one in

I can no longer care so much for it is killing me

This is the only way to survive

World you have won, I surrender

6

Fade

The dragon was slain
But the man full of pain
He couldn't escape
He wasn't too great
The demon was gone
But the woman couldn't move on
She was stuck in the past
She knew this would last
The life was new
The pain was few

RACHAEL ROXANNE VAUGHN

The memories were not
But soon they'd be forgot

7

Escape

I leave you now
I leave you here
I contemplate the fear
I hear the voices
I leave you near
I leave you though
I leave what I cannot grasp
I've tried
This hand
This clasp

I leave the known
for the unknown
I leave the real
for the escape
this is how I survive
This is how I cope
it may not be best
it may not be right
It is what it is

8

It's Relative

Time travel
They say it isn't real
But I've known it
I have lived in another time
I have lived a century
Maybe a thousand centuries
My bones are tired
My past self is almost forgotten
Here I am
Expected to live again

RACHAEL ROXANNE VAUGHN

Expected to face life with all the vigor
of youth

Yet my youth seems an ancient story

I have lived a lifetime already

Yet I know nothing

9

Trapped

Loneliness.
We are one.
I am it and it is me.
It came to me years ago.
It brought gifts then.
Beauty in solitude.
Peace of mind.
Discoveries of me.
But it lingered too long.
It wove its essence into every cell.

It became equally wanted and
equally despised.

It's better this way.

It tells me.

They tell me.

I tell me.

You always find yourself here.

The world doesn't want you.

Only your children do.

You will always be outside looking in.

Just accept me.

We can be best friends.

I tried cutting you out.

I tried silencing you.

But you won't shut the fuck up.

I guess you're right.

You're the best friend I've ever had.

You never go away.

10

Tired

It's certainly strange
This life is weird
Don't know what I'm doing
It's worse than I feared
I wish I had more words
To share how it seems
This is it for tonight
Now's the time for dreams

11

Enough

Gymnastics
The mental kind
Twist it
Turn it
It doesn't fit
Never will
Never was
Never should
Never could
Drop it

Just drop it
Stop it
Shut it
Quit it
One more line
One more time
One more lie
Once more
Three times a charm
Nah

12

Glass Box

Disconnection.

Disassociation.

Disappearing.

Living in a lonely alternate dimension.

Time moves more slowly here.

It's a strange thing, always longing to join the rest of humanity, but not knowing quite how.

13

Closure

He thieved my heart away
And ran off with it
Never to give it back
Never to tell me why
Now I am forever stuck there
A prisoner of my memory
And he is married and happy
Will I ever be?
He holds the key
He can just tell me what happened

RACHAEL ROXANNE VAUGHN

What kind of person can't let another be free?

14

Yummy

Slither
Slither
Slither
Slowly
I crawl
Must escape
Dark
Bloody
Dense
What creature is this?

A slurp
and a smack?
Run, run, run
I can't, I must
I'm stuck
Twisting
Lurching
Stumbling
Ah! It's a feast
It smiles
It stands
"Just in time"

15

Words Unsaid

It's easy for you to be happy all the time.

It's easy for you to not be burdened with others' pain and suffering.

You never take your rose-colored glasses off.

I guess you've never had to.

You stay in your own bubble where anything "negative," is rejected.

You live in a dreamland devoid of truth.

Every hope you've had, every desire for your life, has and continues to be filled.

Then you turn around and ask me what my problem is.

You wonder what's "wrong" with me.

Why can't I simply choose to be like you, to look at the world as you do.

Life's not that hard, or at least it shouldn't be, you say.

All you have to do is decide to be positive no matter what. It's easy.

Of course it's easy for you.

You've been surrounded by love and good people all your life, according to what you tell me.

You've had nourishment, family, community.

And I'm so happy for you, so fiercely happy for you.

I just wish you knew that has been so hard to find for so many.

If only we were all that lucky, then what a wonderful world it would be.

But experience shapes us, and our experiences are as vast as the deepest chasm.

You have no clue of my world, but how could you?

It's not your fault. It just is what it is.

So as much as I wish you knew what my world has been like and continues to be,

I am so glad, so very glad you haven't actually known.

I'm just sad that for so many this is true...our lives, our personalities, our minds, our hearts, our souls have been marred so drastically, altered so markedly by that relentless force called life and those in it, that we may as well live on another planet.

There will always be those who distance themselves, who walk away because they don't understand, because our truth is filled with far more harsh reality and "craziness" than they care to face.

But does that mean my truth doesn't deserve to be heard?

Does that mean I should be rejected by "polite" society?

Will I always be viewed as too, too, too much?

Do you think I can't feel or acknowledge, or experience joy too?

That I don't appreciate the beauty and love, and pure wonder that is also part of life?

I can, I have, and I do, and probably more acutely and vividly than you'd imagine.

But must I only acknowledge the good, and bury the bad?

Must I only present the normal?

Must I hide the other?

Must I lie to you? To myself, and to the world?

No, I cannot. I can only ever be true to myself,

and I'm sorry that's not good enough for you.

SPRING

16

Love Is

Love is dynamic, able to bend, twist and turn

Love expands infinitely to hold all that a person could ever be

Love is surrender to another and in that beautiful surrender, you find all the freedom you ever dreamed of

Love is selfless and in that selflessness you gain all you could wish for

Love is never still, love is never false, love is never ceasing

Love is finding all you thought you lost

Love is too deep for words

Love is not as scary as we think

Love is peeling back layer after layer, secret after secret, desire after desire until you are naked and vulnerable

And right when you think all is lost, you find that you are loved even more deeply than you thought possible

17

You

Moments in time
We've only a few
And in this rhyme
I finally found you
Wishes come and go
Many fade
Some glow
Others you trade
Do wishes come true?
In real life

SEASONS AND MUSINGS

Most never do
Then comes strife
But sometimes magic
Seeps from dreams
Replacing all the tragic
Not all is what it seems

18

Immemorial

To have and to hold
To love and cherish
One soul, one heart
Beauty and laughter untold
Forever til we perish
A precious secret locked away
A notion so dear
An idea pure from the start
Eagerly awaiting that day
When all shall hear

Of a story to set the soul free

Of treasures so sweet

Of song only tender affection can impart

Delights so cherished by me

Are they hidden in those I meet?

A heart quickly taken

Precariously flies about

Looking for the one who made it depart

To another can it ever awaken?

And once again sing, dance, and shout?

For the thief can the victim wait?

A prisoner of the strangest kind

Its capture a well perfected art

Kindness and love being the bait

Never a sweeter criminal shall you find

An ancient tale with a beginning so brief

Whose pages shall be turned forever more

Heard by near and now and worlds apart

Whispered tree to tree, leaf by leaf

Born of past and delivered to future's shore

19

Disappearing Act

Forever and a day
That's what I want
Here and there
That's what I get
Poof
Love arrives
Poof
Love leaves
One day
Maybe

RACHAEL ROXANNE VAUGHN

Who knows?
Love will stay
Will it be you?

20

Compassion

Compassion is the nurse who goes out of their way to help you feel safe and secure during your first (and very scary) psych ward stay.

Compassion is the new acquaintance you've made promptly offering you a bed and a home when you've been living out of your car.

Compassion is the coworker turned friend subtly, consistently, and lovingly planting the seeds that will eventually enable you to see that you have in fact, been born into a cult, and are being abused, manipulated, and used by your so-called physical and spiritual "family."

Compassion is the stranger who sees you sobbing at the back of the metro bus and comes over to offer a hug and an ear.

Compassion is the ex who pays your rent for you because you're about to be evicted.

Compassion is the friend who physically and literally stops you from doing something reckless because you have no will left to live in utter pain and terror any longer.

Compassion is life sending me angels at these crucial moments to show me the compassion I was deprived of for more than two decades of my life. There are so many moments of compassion, big and small, that one is shown throughout their lifetimes, but these are the ones that stand out to me because without every SINGLE one of these acts of compassion, I feel quite strongly that I wouldn't be alive today.

Compassion is the recipient of compassion bestowing compassion on the next soul, and so on and so on.

Compassion is the one rarely shown compassion bestowing compassion on the next soul because they don't want anyone to know the pain of being unloved. Compassion is an everlasting quality and gift we can give to one another. Though many things change, compassion is here to stay.

21

You and I

Let's share a daydream
you and I
I know we already do
You think of me
And I think of you
Let our hearts connect
across time and space
Let's make this daydream real
you and I
Why not?

Let go of your fear
I am not afraid
Let's cross into the realms of the real
you and I
I am waiting
Where are you?

22

Daughter

Watching her smile
Hearing her laughter
Nothing beats it
Precious
Sweet
Curious
A handful
But a good one

23

New

A new day
A new life
Starts small
One day at a time
Then one day you'll shine
Don't lose faith
Don't escape
Cling to those moments
That make you smile
And after a while

RACHAEL ROXANNE VAUGHN

The new dawn comes

24

Eternal

There's a pulse
in everything
in everything
a voice
A passion
Undying
Unyielding
Erupting
Feel it
Hand to heart

RACHAEL ROXANNE VAUGHN

Ear to nature
Soul to soul

25

Beautiful

I'm not me
I'm not who you said I'd be
I'm not sure what happens next
I'm not sure what is best
I'm not me of the past
I'm not me you saw last
I'm not sure who I am
I'm not sure where I land
I'm finally sure of this
I'm sure it's what you all miss

RACHAEL ROXANNE VAUGHN

I'm sure that we must all see
Then we can all be free
I finally see that I am beautiful.

SUMMER

26

Summer

Hey all you children at heart
Here's a good place to start
More fun, more fun
More sun, more sun
That's my mantra for summer
Leave no space for bummer
Makes a nice recipe for happy
Don't let this season be sappy

27

Cloud 19

Slurriness

Blurriness

Fogginess

What day is it? Ah who knows, go back to sleep...

...wait is slurriness even a word? Who cares, this is cloud 19.

The Orb

I walked out in the night
Suddenly there was a light
It was perfect, this orb
Wisdom I needed to absorb
Breathless I reached out
Still filled with doubt
What would I receive?
What trace would it leave?
It drew ever so near
Spoke almost too quietly to hear

SEASONS AND MUSINGS

"Guess what?
Chicken butt"

29

What is This?

Bibbity bobitty boo
another day, another poem
oooh what shall I do?
just have to show 'em
Show them what you goof?
Show them this shit
Stop being a doof
This ain't it
Listen, listen, you
You can just have some fun

When your brain is in the loo
So c'mon hun
Laugh with me for kicks
at the nonsense mush
flipping floppy flicks
Slipping sloppy shush

30

Here

There are no walls
Only a white emptiness
My hand runs along air
I hear voices
Unknown
Unclear
Whispers and echoes
Wishes and laughter
Secrets and scars
A presence

Over there
I turn and stare
Behind me
No to the left
I drift and I feel light
I walk along the non-edge
Of this no-floor
I am soothed
I know not where I am
I only know I want to stay

31

Learn

The children see
what we've forgot
What can it be
What was it we sought?
They do not fear
Voices of love, light
Is all they hear
With it they don't fight
We make them doubt
We dampen the noise

We make them shout
We don't act with poise
There is much to learn
From these gifts
But first trust we must earn
And all the darkness lifts

32

Acceptance

Passing time
Missing rhyme
Does it count anyway?
Always felt that dismay
Where is it now?
Not here, but how?
Today I am happy
Not to be sappy
It comes and goes
When no one knows

SEASONS AND MUSINGS

So all day sit with this
No need to question bliss

33

Existence

Here's a short one
To pass the time
That's what we do
Sometimes
It's too dull
This life
We kick up trouble
To save ourselves
From the mundane

34

Inner Child

There was once
A little girl
Where, you say?
In me
This little girl
She's there still
Laughing and teasing
Creating and dreaming
This little girl
Reminds me to never

RACHAEL ROXANNE VAUGHN

Grow too old
Only just enough to get by
This little girl
Will always be by my side
I must nurture her
I must trust her
This little girl
Helps me find my way
When I'm lost
She never leads me astray

35

Home

Here where I belong
I breathe the ocean air
I let the sandy water
flow through my open fingers
My heart feels
The wisdom in these waters
The peace and love
Inherent and overflowing
Is ever present in such serenity
Return to me

RACHAEL ROXANNE VAUGHN

Come home
Each wave calls
The time is not yet
But it's certain
And it's beautiful
And it's perfect

FALL

36

Only Now

There it is once more
That fleeting echo
I never could find a door
Nothing but a soft yellow
What will become
Of all the memory
Can we save some
Create a treasury
The last humans remain
What becomes then?

SEASONS AND MUSINGS

How do we all gain?
We know it all ends, but when?
I pulled out my soul
We talked as friends do
It's seen all there is to know
There really is nothing new
The mystery is vast
That conscious landscape
That future, the past
Never took shape

37

That Life

The more I let go
The more I gain
That life
It is over
Freedom, freedom, freedom
What will you do with it?
Be glad for freedom
Don't keep yourself chained
Mourn the good you lost
Happily release the ugly

Your voice
use it
you have a voice
You have something to say
It needs the light
It needs to be heard
You have a voice
many will be glad to know

38

In The Box

Put it away
Put it away
It's not happening again
How could it?
Put it away
He's gone
The moment is over
You can't relive it
Put it away
Don't search for that feeling

Don't look for something that can't be
Don't waste what's in front of you
for a memory
Put it away
You can love again
You just can't have that love again
Don't be sad, it's okay
Put it away
It was beautiful
It was forever
Now preserve it
And put him away
Put him away Rachael
Let him go
Give yourself some peace

39

Whispers

There is a sound
a quiet one
I often hear
Within I am found
Without I am done
There is a voice
That calls to me
When night does appear
It all presents a choice
What life wants us to be

SEASONS AND MUSINGS

There is a song
Whose melody is sweet
Draws me near
I feel all I long for
it makes me complete
There is a story
As yet unfinished
Takes away my fear
Love in all its glory
Truth never diminished
There is a cry
too deep for words
That makes it all clear
Healing to die
Pain transferred

40

A Moment of Truth

A moment of truth
clears the hazy fog
Now you can breathe
as you're lifted from the bog
The sorrows, the hurts
the questions, the regrets
have they all led to this?
To the place one often forgets
Hailing from ages long ago
voices that have known a better day

faintly reaches ears that are ill used
to remind us there is a different way
A fire lit within the soul
All is silent, all is new
The heart is soothed
if only for a few
Noise seeps in again
it is slipping, fading out
Was it just an illusion?
Come back, don't leave me in doubt
Just a flicker of light
too brief, too small
Only a fragrant whiff
of the secret of it all

41

Wishing

Waiting, waiting
always debating
Is the time now?
Yes, but how?
How do I cope
without much hope
of seeing the one I miss?
The one I long to kiss

42

I Forgot

Oh my gosh
I forgot!
This phrase
I say it a lot!
Forgetful
Never used to be me
Forgetful
I hate that word
Forgetful

RACHAEL ROXANNE VAUGHN

I wish I could forget the things I remember

And remember the things I forget

43

Birthday

Thirty-five

Still mixed up inside

My mind showed wear and tear long ago

Now my body does so

Egads! Have I joined

the ranks of the old?

Nah, I'm just wiser

so I'm told

Ah yes I'm now

RACHAEL ROXANNE VAUGHN

All-knowing
Having lived, loved, and lost
Isn't my maturity showing?
Ecstasy, wonder, terror
Bliss, heartbreak, and pain
Can you blame me if I
got a bit insane?
Lots of chaos and weirdness
in the story of me
But there's lots more to me
You'll see
Sometimes you gotta say
"Well fuck"
Here I go
Wish me luck!

44

Who, Me?

Be you.
Not that you.
Not that one either
No, no, no
You're doing it all wrong
Look at me
Don't you see?
This is how you do it
This is how you fit
You can't come in here

You can't come near
All willy-nilly chaos
Go give yourself a wash
No, I shall baffle
I shall confuse
I shall be wild and free
I shall be me
You shall be you

45

Waiting

It was as if she'd been waiting

And in that waiting was agony

But also a tiny space for hope

And that hope gave way to excitement

The agony of excitement if you will

Of the unknown

Of the future

Of hidden depths

And it brought forth mirth

RACHAEL ROXANNE VAUGHN

It allowed in light and laughter

And at last her mind jauntily traveled with these

and just allowed all things to be

46

Perseverance

Ready to throw in the towel
But holding it tight
I've come so far
I can't stop
Need to know
what lies ahead
Always wondering
Always pondering
Need to get out of my head
Ready to stay

Ready to leave
In need of adventure
Restless soul
Aimless mind
Happy yet am I?
Sad yet not quite
What is this?
Stillness
Acceptance or defeat
It's a fine line
Temporary days
All shall pass
Joy comes soon
Keep on the path

47

Interruption

Circles
Circles
Vicious circles
never-ending
Repeating
Flipping, bending
Break the loop
Break the cycle
Break it
Break it now

RACHAEL ROXANNE VAUGHN

Upend the pattern
Change the course

48

Cherish

These moments

are all we have

Laughing in silliness with my children

I take in every inch of their sweet faces

And a pang, a dull ache ripples through my heart

This too shall pass it says

All is fleeting

All is temporary

RACHAEL ROXANNE VAUGHN

To know such sweetness, such light

Doesn't always last is a fear I'd rather not indulge

I sigh away the fear

and I laugh a bit harder

I squeeze their hands a bit tighter

I say I love you with every breath

And I ease into this paradox

So what can we do?

Love a bit more fiercely

Go after our dreams a bit more brazenly

Laugh a lot louder than maybe need be

and leave a trail of beautiful memories

49

Paper Fragments

Paper fragments
float here and there
I nudged them
I whispered to them
I made them come back
Back to me
You're mine I say
You're mine
Stay
We will be made whole again

RACHAEL ROXANNE VAUGHN

These paper fragments
hold all my shaky breaths
And with each shaky breath
I am slowly coming back to life

50

Becoming You

Yes, sometimes it happens, just like that.

No fanfare, no gimmicks, no huge ah-ha moment.

You've had those moments. Those events.

The "I've lost it all and hit rock bottom" moment.

The "my heart and soul is broken, shattered" moment.

You've had those moments of truth, those life-altering epiphanies.

But you always ended up, eventually, in the same place, with the same mindset.

No, it happens in the calm, in the everyday, taken for granted moments.

The moment, the best feeling, when you're at peace with yourself, and with the world around you.

You look down at your sleeping beauties, one against your shoulder. The other cradled in your arms.

And you sigh with contentment, with the steady, stable feeling of joy.

You wonder how you got so lucky, and you know, without a shadow of a doubt, you will never fall back to the old patterns.

You are a new creature, a phoenix rising from the ashes.

You are light.

You are love.

You are kindness.

All that you have longed for in another soul, is all that you have become.

All's right with the world, at that moment.

And it is just the beginning.

www.ingramcontent.com/pod-product-compliance
Lightning Source LLC
Chambersburg PA
CBHW031947070426
42453CB00007BA/445